Contents

Let's Dream, Martin Luther King, Jr.!

by Peter and Connie Roop

SCHOLASTIC INC.

New York   Toronto   London   Auckland   Sydney
Mexico City   New Delhi   Hong Kong   Buenos Aires

For Hattie, whose love of learning and sense of justice make the world a better place

ISBN 0-439-55443-8

Text copyright © 2004 by Peter and Connie Roop.
Illustrations copyright © 2004 by Scholastic Inc.
All rights reserved. Published by Scholastic Inc.
SCHOLASTIC and associated logos are trademarks and/or registered trademarks of Scholastic Inc.

12 11 10 9 8 7 6 5 4 3 2   4 5 6 7 8 9/0

Printed in the U.S.A.   40
First printing, January 2004

Introduction

Dr. Martin Luther King, Jr., made history. He became famous for his work helping African Americans get equal rights. Do you know that Martin Luther King was given a different name when he was born?

Martin Luther King, Jr., was very active as a boy. Did you know he almost died in an accident?

Martin Luther King, Jr., loved to play football. Do you know what other sports he played?

Martin Luther King, Jr., grew up to be a Baptist minister. Do you know what other careers he considered?

Martin Luther King, Jr., worked hard to make sure laws were fair for all Americans, especially African Americans. Did you know Dr. King broke unfair laws and went to jail many times?

Dr. King gave hundreds of speeches. Do you know what his most famous speech was?

Dr. King worked hard to settle problems peacefully. Do you know what famous award he received for his work?

The answers to these questions lie in who Martin Luther King, Jr., was as a boy and as a young man. This book is about Martin Luther King, Jr., before he made history.

1
Martin Luther King, Jr., Is Born

Saturday, January 15, 1929, was a chilly day in Atlanta, Georgia. But inside the yellow house at 501 Auburn Street, it was a happy day for Mike and Alberta King. Their first son had been born.

The doctor worried that something was wrong. The baby was still and quiet. The doctor gently spanked the baby a few times. The baby cried, his powerful voice heard for the very first time.

His parents named their son Michael Luther King, Jr., after his father, Michael Luther King, Sr. But before long he was

called M. L. so that he would not be confused with his father, Mike.

M. L.'s grandparents, Reverend and Mrs. A. D. Williams, smiled at their grandson. The new baby would share a home with his parents and his sister, Christine.

That night, baby Mike King slept in his parents' room in Christine's old wooden crib.

M. L.'s father, Mike King, Sr., was a minister. He had not had an easy life growing up. He had lived on a poor farm in Georgia. He went to a separate school for African-American children. He plowed, planted, and harvested crops. He took care of the family mule.

Mike saw that many white people had better jobs and more money than African Americans. He wondered why white people had things that his family did not have. Mike saw that many white people treated African Americans unfairly. He had seen African Americans beaten by white men. Once a white man hit Mike for not bringing him water to drink.

When he was fifteen years old, Mike King made a decision. He wanted a better life for himself, so he left the farm. Mike walked to Atlanta, Georgia, with his only pair of shoes dangling over his shoulder to save the leather.

Along the way, Mike saw the nice brick house of a white banker. Mike promised himself that one day he and his family would live in a brick house, too.

When Mike got to Atlanta he did hard jobs. He worked in a shop repairing machines and as a railroad fireman. There were not many good jobs for African Americans.

Mike King had a dream, however. He enjoyed going to church. He liked to listen to the preachers and their messages. He knew that church ministers were respected leaders in the African-American community. Mike felt that God wanted him to be a minister, too. But first he must finish high school.

Mike went to night school to earn his high school diploma. He also worked in two churches. He would preach one Sunday in one church and preach the next Sunday in the other church.

In 1926, Mike went to Morehouse College in Atlanta to earn a college degree. There, Mike met Alberta Williams. Her father, Reverend A. D. Williams, was pastor of the Ebenezer Baptist Church in Atlanta. Before long, Mike and Alberta fell in love. They were married on Thanksgiving Day, 1926.

Mike King became the assistant pastor at Ebenezer Baptist Church. Mike and Alberta had little money, so they lived upstairs in the Williams's yellow-and-brown house on Auburn Street. This is where Christine King was born, in 1927. This is also where Michael Luther King, Jr., was born. No one knew it then, but one day quiet M. L. would grow up to be Dr. Martin Luther King, Jr., a man whose voice would be heard around the world.

2
Mike King, Jr., Gets a New Name

In 1931, when M. L. was two years old, his grandfather A. D. Williams died. M. L. missed his grandfather, but he still had plenty of family to love him: his father and mother, his grandmother, his sister, Christine, and his younger brother, Alfred Daniel, who was called A. D.

M. L.'s father became pastor of the Ebenezer Baptist Church. He worked hard to get more people to join his church. Soon the church had to build more rooms to hold everyone.

M. L. was too young to understand the

problems of African Americans. There were many unfair laws against them that had been made to keep African Americans and white people separate. These laws were called Jim Crow laws. Keeping people of different races or backgrounds apart is called segregation.

All over the South, Jim Crow laws kept African Americans and white people separated from one another. White people sat downstairs at movies, while African Americans had to sit in the balcony. White people had their own bathrooms and drinking fountains that African Americans were not allowed to use. African Americans had to sit or stand at the back of a bus. If a white person wanted to sit down, an African American had to give up his or her seat. African-American children could not go to school with white children. African Americans received lower pay for doing the same jobs as white people.

M. L.'s father did not like Jim Crow laws because they hurt African Americans. He tried to change the laws. He would not ride a bus. He worked so that teachers, African-American and white, received better pay. He took a special reading test just for African Americans so he could vote. He led African Americans on a march so that more African Americans would be able to vote.

M. L. was too young to understand these unfair laws. But as he grew older, he saw how his people suffered.

One day, when M. L. was four years old, his parents drove through Atlanta. All over America, people had lost their jobs during the Depression. In Atlanta, more than half of the African Americans had no work. M. L. was very upset when he saw a long line of poor African Americans.

M. L. asked why the people were in line. His mother explained that they were hungry. They were waiting in line to get free food. M. L. worried that the children would not get enough to eat.

From an early age, M. L. loved words. He surrounded himself with books even before he could read. He enjoyed the stories his grandmother told about her childhood. He especially liked it when she read stories about faraway places.

M. L. liked Bible stories, too. M. L. memorized parts of the Bible and repeated them. He memorized songs. His mother and grandmother were very proud of M. L. They often told him how wonderful and smart he was. M. L. beamed with this praise.

M. L. said, "You just wait and see. When I grow up, I'm going to get me some big words."

In 1934, when M. L. was five years old, he was in church, sitting beside his grandmother and his sister. A visiting preacher gave the sermon. His father, Reverend King, sat near the pulpit. His mother played the organ. The preacher asked if anyone wanted to join the church that day. Christine leaped up to join. M. L. did not want his sister to do anything better than he could, so he jumped up and joined the church, too.

The church had always been important in the life of the King family. Reverend King made a decision. He changed his first name to Martin to honor Martin Luther, a famous Christian leader. Reverend King changed M. L.'s first name, too. M. L. was no longer Michael Luther King, Jr. Now he was Martin Luther King, Jr. But his friends still called him M. L.

3

"Martin, You Are Somebody!"

When Martin was five years old, his parents thought he was ready for school. They sent him to first grade. When the teacher asked him how old he was, M. L. answered, "Five years old." M. L. was very honest. The teacher told M. L. to come back next year when he was six.

M. L. liked to play inside. His favorite board game was Monopoly. He played Chinese checkers and marbles. He built buildings with toy logs.

Outside, he played tag with Christine and A. D. He played baseball and football in his backyard with his African-American and white friends. He flew kites. He rode his bike around the block. He built a tree house with A. D.

Sometimes M. L. was careless. Twice he was accidentally hit by cars. But luckily, he was not hurt! One time, M. L. fell over the banister at the top of the stairs, hit the first floor, and rolled into the basement. He wasn't hurt that time, either! Another time, M. L. was playing baseball. A. D. swung the bat and accidentally hit M. L. in the head. M. L. wasn't hurt. He said later that God must have been protecting him from being injured in all those accidents.

M. L. and A. D. sometimes got into trouble. One day M. L. and A. D. were sliding down the banister. A. D. slid down just as Grandmother Williams entered the hall. A. D. crashed into her and knocked her out!

M. L. thought they had killed her! He was so upset that he jumped out an upstairs window. M. L. fell twelve feet to the ground. He heard people yell his name, but he didn't answer. But when he heard someone say that his grandmother was not hurt, M. L. acted as though nothing had happened.

M. L., Christine, and A. D. liked to trick people. One day they took their grandmother's fur scarf that looked like a fox. They tied the fur to a stick and hid with it in the bushes. When someone walked down the sidewalk, they poked out the fur. The surprised person sometimes jumped and yelled. The children laughed in their hiding place.

Martin liked to play the piano, but he didn't always enjoy the lessons. Mr. Mann, the piano teacher, rapped M. L.'s knuckles if he didn't play well. M. L. and A. D. decided to trick Mr. Mann.

Before Mr. Mann arrived at their house, the boys unscrewed the legs of the piano bench. When Mr. Mann sat down, the legs shot out from under the bench, and he toppled to the floor! Another time, when M. L. got tired of playing the piano, he took a hammer and chipped the middle C key.

M. L. had chores to do. In the winter, he

shoveled coal into the furnace to warm the house. He tapped the temperature gauge with his foot so that enough heat would come upstairs. He was supposed to help Christine do the dishes, but often he hid in the bathroom to escape this job.

M. L. got an allowance of twenty-five cents if he did his chores. He saved some money, gave money to his church, and spent the rest on candy!

M. L. had many African-American and white friends. His best friends were two white boys whose parents owned a grocery store across the street from M. L.'s house.

One day, when he was six years old, M. L. went to get his white friends to play ball in M. L.'s big backyard. The boys' parents said that their sons could no longer play with M. L. When M. L. asked why, the adults said, "Because we are white and you are colored (African-American)."

That night at dinner, M. L. sadly told his parents what had happened and how he could no longer play with his friends. His

parents told M. L. that many African Americans had once been slaves and had been owned by white people. They told him how Abraham Lincoln and the Civil War had ended slavery, but now there were Jim Crow laws to keep white people and African Americans apart.

M. L. thought about the school where he and Christine went. There were no white children there. The white children went to another, better school.

His mother told M. L. something he never forgot. She said, "You must never feel that you are less than anybody else. You must always feel that you are somebody!"

Still, M. L. was very angry. He wanted to hate every white person, but he was too nice to really hate anyone.

4
Martin Learns
More Lessons

M. L. was still upset by the unfairness of African-American life in Atlanta. He couldn't buy a soft drink at stores because he was African American. Because he was African American, he could not eat a meal at a lunch counter that served white people. When he bought ice cream from the window marked COLORED ONLY, his was served in a paper cup, not in a dish like the ice cream for white people. He could go to school, but not to a school with white children.

M. L. experienced these unfair things and did not like them. He especially did not like the signs reading WHITES ONLY in shops,

swimming pools, libraries, restaurants, parks, hotels, and in waiting rooms at train and bus stations. Though M. L. did not like these unfair laws, there was nothing he could do to change them.

M. L. felt safe and protected with his family. He respected his parents very much. He was proud of the way his father stood up to white people who tried to put him down.

One day, M. L. and his father were driving in Atlanta. A white police officer stopped Reverend King and said, "Boy, show me your license."

Reverend King said, "Do you see this child here?"

The police officer looked at M. L.

"That's a boy," Reverend King said. "I'm a man."

M. L.'s father told him, "When I stand up, I want everybody to know that a man is standing."

One time, M. L. went to buy new shoes with his father. The shopkeeper made them sit in the back because they were African

American. Reverend King refused and said, "We'll either buy shoes sitting here, or we won't buy any shoes at all." M. L. and his father left the store empty-handed.

M. L. learned another big lesson from his father. He learned that the segregation system was unfair to African Americans and that he did not have to accept it.

Reverend King said, "I don't care how long I have to live with the system, I am never going to accept it. I'll fight it until I die." Young M. L. took these words to heart.

M. L. also learned many lessons in school. From first grade to fifth grade, he went to Younge Street Elementary School. He usually worked hard and was polite to his teachers and fellow students. In sixth grade, M. L. went to David T. Howard Colored Elementary School. Even if his school was for African-American children only, M. L. was determined to be somebody.

When M. L. was too upset by the unfair laws, he had someone at home who helped him — his loving grandmother, Mama. Mama comforted M. L., told him stories, and read him books. She gave M. L. lots of love, which he returned to her.

When he was twelve years old, M. L.'s life changed. On May 14, 1941, M. L. had grown tired of studying and went outside to watch an African-American parade. While M. L. was enjoying the parade, someone told him that something had happened to his grandmother. M. L. rushed home to learn that his beloved Mama had died from a heart attack.

M. L. mistakenly thought he had caused Mama's death. He had left his important studies to enjoy a parade. M. L. was so upset that he ran upstairs and jumped out a window! He was hurt, but did not die.

Day after day, M. L. cried for Mama. Night after night, M. L. tossed and turned. He couldn't sleep. M. L.'s parents comforted him. They told him Mama's death was not his fault. They told him God chose when someone's life was to end. They told M. L. that he would always have Mama's warm encouragement and powerful love.

5
Martin Learns
a Bitter Lesson

Late in 1941, Reverend King's dream came true. As a young man he had promised himself that someday he would live in a nice brick house. Reverend King found a two-story redbrick house on Boulevard, and the Kings moved.

M. L. made new friends in his neighborhood. He played baseball, basketball, and football with an energy that puzzled his friends. When he played baseball, no one could tell if he was playing for fun or in anger. When he played basketball, M. L. wouldn't pass the ball. He took shots whenever he had the ball. His friends wanted him to play quarterback in football. But M. L. knocked people down whenever he had the football, so they let him play fullback instead.

M. L. sometimes got into fights. At first, he used his skill with words to argue with his opponent. If arguing didn't work, M. L. said, "Let's go to the grass." M. L. could outwrestle anyone he met.

Even if he was rough and tough in sports, M. L. still loved to learn. He worked hard. In 1942, when M. L. was thirteen years old, he went to Booker T. Washington High School. He enjoyed reading, writing, and math. In high school, he plunged into his favorite subjects, English and history.

As M. L. read, he thought. He tried to understand how some writers shared their thoughts powerfully through words. When he was younger, M. L. wanted "big words." Now he had them, and he knew where to get more.

M. L. memorized speeches and documents. He was already skilled with the language and rhythms of the Bible. He combined these old words with his new words.

As much as M. L. loved words, he had trouble spelling. At night, M. L. and Christine studied together. Math was easy for Martin, so he helped Christine with her math homework. Christine helped Martin with his spelling. M. L. said, "I can't spell a lick." M. L. remembered many powerful words, but not how to spell them.

M. L. loved music. He played the piano and violin. He listened to opera on the family's record player. He sang in church and at home.

In 1943, when Martin was fourteen years old, his voice changed. Martin's voice was now a deep baritone. People listened when Martin talked, sang, or argued.

His parents, friends, and teachers encouraged Martin to speak out and show his love of words. In 1944, when he was in the eleventh grade, Martin wrote a speech titled "The Negro and the Constitution." Martin practiced and practiced until the words rolled off his tongue. With his teacher's help, Martin entered a speech contest in another Georgia town.

Martin and his teacher rode a bus to the town. Martin gave his speech and won a prize for his strong, convincing "big words." Martin was pleased. He was eager to share his success with his family.

On the bus ride home, Martin and his teacher talked about the success of his speech. The day had been long. The ride home was long, too. But it felt good to sit down and talk.

Along the way, the bus stopped to pick up more passengers. Soon, the bus was full. Two white passengers got onto the bus. They looked for seats, but there were none. The white bus driver ordered Martin and his teacher to give their seats to the two white passengers.

Martin said, "No!"

The bus driver said, "Yes!"

Martin would not move. At last, his

teacher convinced Martin to move so there wouldn't be trouble.

Later, Martin wrote, "That night will never leave my mind. It was the angriest I have ever been in my life."

6

Martin's First Sermon

Martin turned his energies to his school-work. He studied so hard that he skipped twelfth grade and graduated from high school in 1944, when he was only fifteen years old.

Much of America's attention was focused on World War II. Martin was too young to be a soldier, so he decided to go to college. Martin was accepted at Morehouse College in Atlanta, where his father had gone. Martin would begin classes in the fall of 1944.

Before he went to college, Martin wanted to work in a northern state. Martin and several other Morehouse students rode a train to Connecticut to work in the tobacco fields.

This was the first time Martin had been away from his family.

Martin and his friends worked hard, weeding, watering, and caring for the tobacco plants. The days were long and hot. Martin didn't mind. He wanted to do real work before returning to his books.

Martin especially liked the weekends, when he and his friends went to Hartford, Connecticut. Hartford was very different from Atlanta. Martin could go to a restaurant serving white people and be served, too. He could go to a movie and sit wherever he liked!

Martin felt a sense of freedom that he had never enjoyed before. But Martin lost this freedom on the train ride home. As the train passed through Connecticut, New York, and New Jersey, Martin sat and ate where he wanted to. But when the train entered Virginia, the segregation laws were enforced. Martin had to sit at a special table for African Americans only.

A waiter pulled a curtain around Martin's

table so the white passengers couldn't see him. Martin felt like "the curtain had dropped on his selfhood."

Martin had to do something to change these humiliating and unfair laws. But what could he do? He was only fifteen years old.

In the fall of 1944, when Martin began college, he wrestled with that question. He could be a minister like his father and grandfather. *No*, he thought. Since the laws were unfair, he would become a lawyer and fight the laws. He stood in front of a mirror and practiced giving speeches in his rich, deep voice.

Martin changed his mind again. He would be a doctor and help keep African Americans healthy.

Martin joined the college football team. He joined the glee club, too — his strong baritone voice was a welcome addition.

Then Martin changed his mind again. This happened when he learned that although he was very smart, he could read only at an eighth-grade level. Martin was angry. He knew this was because he had gone to separate schools for African Americans. These schools didn't have as much money as white schools. The books were older, and there were fewer teaching materials.

Martin studied even harder and got A's in history, philosophy, English, and sociology (how people live together). Martin decided to get his college degree in sociology.

Dr. Benjamin Mays was one of Martin's favorite professors. He taught Martin to "do whatever you do so well that no man living could do it better." Dr. Mays inspired Martin to become a preacher.

When he was seventeen years old, Martin Luther King, Jr., decided to follow in his father's and grandfather's footsteps. He would become a Baptist minister.

When Martin told his father of his decision, Reverend King gave him a test. He told Martin he could preach at Ebenezer Baptist Church, but only in a small room with a small audience.

Martin began his sermon one Sunday

morning. The room filled up. More people came to hear this powerful new preacher. So many people came that Martin and his audience had to move to a big auditorium! Martin Luther King, Jr.'s, first sermon was a tremendous success. In 1947, seventeen-year-old Martin was ordained a minister.

7
Martin's Big Decisions

Martin enjoyed college. During the summer vacations, however, he wanted a different challenge.

Martin had grown up in a loving family. He had food to eat, clothes to wear, and a comfortable home. He said, "I was about to conclude that life had been wrapped up for me in a Christmas present."

Martin felt that something was missing in his life. He wanted to learn how poor people worked and lived. So during the hot and humid summers, Martin took hard jobs that required him to use the strength of his muscles. He worked at the Parkway Express Company unloading boxes from trucks and trains.

Martin sweated and his arms hurt, and he now knew how many of his fellow African Americans toiled to earn a living. But Martin had his pride. One day, when his white boss called him a name, Martin quit.

He took another hard, hot job. He worked for a mattress company, loading and unloading mattresses and box springs. Here, Martin learned another tough lesson. He and the other African Americans worked very hard, but they were paid less than white workers doing the same job.

Martin felt this was unfair. But he didn't know how he could change things. He just knew he had to do something, someday.

When he returned to college, Martin studied even harder. In one class, Martin learned about Henry David Thoreau. Thoreau's solution against unfair laws was not to fight back but to be nonviolent and go to jail for his beliefs. Thoreau believed that "one honest man," even if he stood alone for his beliefs, could change the world. Martin wondered if such nonviolent resistance could help African Americans change the hated Jim Crow segregation laws.

Martin was still angry with many white people. He felt the hurt of not being able to eat in any restaurant or use any bathroom or live in any neighborhood. He hurt for being made to sit in the back of the bus just because of the color of his skin.

Martin became a school leader. He joined a group of students from African-American and white colleges. He realized that not all white people supported the unfair laws. He realized that not all white people hated African Americans. He saw that when people of both races were treated equally, they could work together.

Martin made a decision. He knew he couldn't wait for others to change the laws. He would be in the heat of the battle for equal rights for all Americans.

But Martin wondered what he could do. He was only nineteen years old. Martin decided to keep learning. He would go to another college and learn more about being a minster.

Martin remembered how fairly he had been treated in Connecticut. He decided that he did not want to go to divinity school in Atlanta. He would go north, where he would be treated more equally.

Martin chose Crozer Seminary near Philadelphia, Pennsylvania. Crozer Seminary had only one hundred students. In the fall of 1948, when he was nineteen years old, Martin enrolled at Crozer.

Martin enjoyed the beautiful campus. He liked his fellow students, who came from many different religious backgrounds. Although only six students were African Americans, Martin didn't feel left out.

Martin learned about Mahatma Gandhi. Gandhi, like Thoreau, believed in nonviolence as a way to change unfair laws. Gandhi practiced his nonviolent beliefs in India. Through nonviolent protests and going to jail, Gandhi and his followers helped India

become independent from Great Britain. Gandhi became Martin's hero.

Martin studied so hard that he was the best student in his class. He was elected class president, and he was given money to go to another college and earn his doctor's degree in religion. Martin went to Boston, Massachusetts, to study at Boston University. There, his life changed forever.

8

Martin Becomes a Leader

In February 1952, Martin met Coretta Scott, from Alabama. Coretta was studying to become a concert singer.

Martin took Coretta out to lunch, and he talked and talked. He talked about everything from southern food to music. He even told Coretta, "The four things I look for in a wife are character, intelligence, personality, and beauty. You have them all."

Coretta was not so sure about Martin. She had worked hard to become a concert singer. She did not want to give up her career dreams.

Martin was persuasive. In the summer of 1953, when he was twenty-four years old, Martin and Coretta were married in her fam-

Alabama. But because they were
Americans, they couldn't stay in a lo-
hotel. Martin and Coretta spent their first
married night together in the guest room of a
funeral home.

A year later, Martin finished his classes at
Boston University. When he completed his
final paper he would be Dr. Martin Luther
King, Jr.

Martin and Coretta enjoyed living in the
north where the laws treated them more
equally. But they knew that African Americans' biggest problems were in the southern
states where they had both grown up.

After much discussion with Coretta, Martin accepted a job as the pastor of the Dexter
Avenue Baptist Church in Montgomery, Alabama. Martin worked hard at his new job.
He got up early to write and memorize his
sermons. He practiced speaking to the bathroom mirror! He helped church friends and
families. He spoke at marriages and funerals.
He joined groups working to make life better
for African Americans.

He finished his last college paper. Now, he really was Dr. Martin Luther King, Jr.! Dr. King's church was so proud of their energetic young minister that they paid him the highest salary of any African-American minister in town.

In November 1955, Coretta and Martin celebrated the birth of their daughter Yolanda. They called her Yoki. Then an event happened that changed Martin and the world.

On December 1, 1955, Rosa Parks, a forty-two-year-old African-American seamstress, got on a bus to go home after a hard day's work. Mrs. Parks was tired. She sat on an aisle seat near the middle of the bus. Three other African Americans sat in the same row.

The bus filled. A white man got on, but there was no seat for him. The bus driver said to Mrs. Parks and the three African Americans beside her, "You folks, I want those seats."

The three other African Americans moved. But not Mrs. Parks. The driver de-

manded that she move. Mrs. Parks softly said, "No."

The bus driver stopped the bus. He had Mrs. Parks arrested, taken to jail, and finger-printed. When word reached the African-American community, people decided to boycott the buses. African Americans would not ride the buses until the unfair bus laws were changed. Who could lead such a boy-cott?

The African-American leaders E. D. Nixon and Reverend Ralph Abernathy knew just the right leader: twenty-six-year-old Dr. Martin Luther King, Jr.

Martin agreed to help but not to lead the boycott. They planned for the bus boycott to begin on Monday, December 5, 1955.

Martin was up early that Monday. He wondered if African Americans would really stop riding the buses. To his surprise, the first three buses that rolled past his house — buses usually filled with African-American riders — were empty!

Martin drove around Montgomery. Sidewalks and cars were filled with African Americans walking or riding to work.

That evening, a meeting was held to keep the boycott going. The African Americans needed someone to lead them through the difficult days ahead. The white people of Montgomery were not pleased with the boycott. Martin had to make a difficult decision. Did he have the strength and courage to lead his people, especially if his family was in danger?

Martin agreed to lead the boycott, saying, "If you think I can render some service, I will."

9
Martin Makes a Difference

That evening, Martin was amazed. One thousand African Americans crowded into his church. More than four thousand African Americans stood outside and listened to him.

Martin said, "We are here this evening for serious business." He urged his audience to be nonviolent in their boycott. He reminded them that they were American citizens. He said, "But the glory of American democracy is the right to protest for right. And if we are wrong, the Supreme Court of this nation is wrong." The crowd cheered and clapped.

For a long time, Martin had wanted to help his people. Now, he had his chance.

Martin was pleased as the boycott grew. Every day, African Americans refused to ride buses. Some walked miles to work. Some rode together in carpools. Some took taxis. One man rode his mule.

The white leaders in Montgomery were now upset. They needed African Americans to ride the buses. Eight out of ten bus riders were African Americans. Without them, the bus company was losing money.

The white leaders refused to change the Jim Crow bus laws. The African Americans refused to ride the buses. Dr. King made speeches, encouraged his people, and gave ideas to keep the boycott going.

Dr. King knew, however, that many white people were angry. Some threatened him on his phone. Dr. King believed that he must not give into his enemies, but that he could win them over to his side by not being violent. Through his years of studying religion, Dr. King came to believe that love was a stronger force than violence. Dr. King said, "We must meet the forces of hate with the

power of love." He was determined to change the laws without violence.

But something terrible happened on the night of January 30, 1956. Dr. King was giving a speech. Coretta and baby Yoki were at home. Coretta heard a loud thump on the porch. She took Yoki to a back room. Suddenly, there was an explosion. Someone had bombed the Kings' house!

Dr. King rushed home. Coretta and Yoki were safe. An angry crowd of African Americans had gathered to seek revenge for the bombing. Dr. King calmed them. He told them to put away their weapons. He said, "I want you to love our enemies." Even when his family had been attacked, Martin Luther King, Jr., wanted a peaceful way to make changes.

The boycott continued. Dr. King and others were arrested. Still, African Americans refused to ride buses. Finally, on November 13, 1956, the Supreme Court, the highest court in the United States, decided that segregation on the Montgomery buses was illegal.

A month later, Dr. King and Rosa Parks boarded a bus. They sat where they wanted to. Dr. King had led the African-American community to victory!

After his success in Montgomery, more people heard about Dr. Martin Luther King, Jr., and his peaceful way to change Jim Crow laws. Soon, Martin was traveling around the country giving speeches. *Time* magazine put Dr. King on its cover! He was becoming more famous every day.

Dr. King now joined with other African-American leaders to work to get equal rights for all African Americans. He wanted all African Americans to be able to vote without paying a special tax or taking a special test. He wanted all African Americans to be able to eat in any restaurant, sleep in any hotel, and use any park, pool, drinking fountain, or bathroom. He wanted all African Americans to be able to sit on any seat on any bus or train.

10
Martin Changes the World

Many white people did not like what Dr. King was doing. Dr. King broke many Jim Crow laws, which he said were unfair. Often when he broke a law, he was arrested and put in jail. Dr. King said, "There comes a time when a moral man can't obey a law which his conscience tells him is unjust."

In 1960, Dr. King decided it was time for him to leave Montgomery and return to Atlanta. He would join his father's church as an assistant pastor. There, he could preach and still work hard for civil rights.

In 1961, President Kennedy invited Dr. King to come to the White House. They talked about national civil rights laws.

Other people were working to change

laws, too. But change was slow. Some African Americans wanted to fight white people. Dr. King urged them to not use violence. He said, "The old law of an eye for an eye leaves everyone blind."

In 1963, Dr. King was invited to Birmingham, Alabama, to fight the segregation laws there. Even though the Supreme Court had decided that segregation laws were illegal on buses and trains, schools, restaurants, parks, and pools, many white people did not agree. Dr. King went to Birmingham to help the African Americans there.

But Dr. King was put in jail in Birmingham. While he sat in his cell, he wrote his famous *Letter from Birmingham Jail*. He had no paper, so he wrote on the edge of a newspaper and on toilet paper. He explained that change must come, but come peacefully. His letter was smuggled out of jail and shared with the world.

Many African Americans were protesting the unfair laws. Many went to jail. Then, on May 2 and 3, 1963, thousands of children marched against the segregation laws. Fire-fighters knocked them down with fire hoses. They were attacked by police dogs. Children as young as six years old were put in jail. But no one fought back.

Newspapers and television programs showed pictures of what happened to these peaceful young people. People across America were angry at how African Americans were being treated. President Kennedy spoke against the segregation laws. Change was coming!

In August 1963, Dr. King stood before 250,000 people in Washington, D.C., and gave his "I Have a Dream" speech. Millions more heard him, on television, say those famous words: "I say to you today, my friends, so even though we face the difficulties of today and tomorrow, I still have a dream. It is a dream deeply rooted in the American dream. I have a dream that one day this nation will rise up and live out the true meaning of its creed: 'We hold these truths to be self-evident;

that all men are created equal.' I have a dream my four little children will one day live in a nation where they will not be judged by their color but by the content of their character. I have a dream today."

Dr. King was now known all around the world. In 1964, he received the Nobel Peace Prize for his work to change unfair laws. But his work was not over. Dr. King gave more speeches, joined more marches, and worked to change more laws. He would not stop dreaming until "little black boys and black girls will be able to join hands with little white boys and white girls as sisters and brothers."

In April 1968, Dr. King went to Memphis, Tennessee, to support African-American sanitation workers. On April 4, while he stood on a motel balcony with friends, a single shot rang out. Dr. King had been shot. He died later that night.

Dr. King's grave is in Atlanta beside his beloved Ebenezer Baptist Church. On his grave are his words, "Free at Last, Free at

Last. Thank God Almighty, I am Free at Last."

Dr. King's dream did not die with him. His dream continues wherever people work to make life better for everyone, anywhere around the world. Who would have known that Martin Luther King, Jr., would change the world when he was born on that January day in 1929?